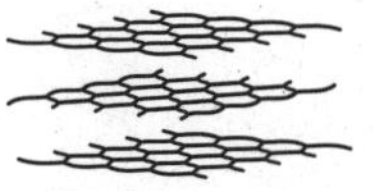

PLAY

PLAY

Liz Waldner

Lightful Press

Published by Lightful Press
www.lightfulpress.com

This book has been composed in Scala and Copperplate.

Cover art by Mollie Goldstrom.
Cover printed at Brown Parcel Press, Brooklyn, NY

Printed in the United States of America on acid-free, recycled, archival paper.

ISBN: 978-0-9822471-0-5

5 4 3 2 1

TABLE OF CONTENTS

I salute Shri Guru, whose two lotus feet remove the pain of duality…
Verse 43, Guru Gita

I saw my Lord with the eye of my heart and I said, "Who art thou?"
He said, "Thou."
al-Hallaj

THE IMAGINED SNAKE IS THE SPORT OF THE ROPE

i.

I say Bora-Bora.

You are not to say Bora-Bora.

I say Bora-Bora for it is one of the names of God.

You are not to say one of the names of God.

I—

You are not able or you are not worthy.

—

You botch or you rot (transitive).

—

Bot-u-lizm.

—

Furthermore you just tried to eat around the rotten part of the apple and failed.

ii.

I say, don't I know you from somewhere?

Who are you?

(song&dance ensue)

iii. Proparoxytonic

"out of the reach of hope"

nobody liked that poem, you know

"*cha(I)ritable*": flesh is the root of mercy

she called that 'word play'   as in 'silly shilly shally'

flesh, mercy: endure, endure

bode well for you abide in a body?

"Love said, then you must taste my meat.
So I did sit and eat": bid, bade, bidden (beat)

iv. Aubade

not that.
(they _______ (verb signifying contempt scorn contumely); therefore I must
      not _____ (be))

not you.
(not: the present moment already made/passed)

v.

I say Bora-Bora.

(How dares the little crocodile)

dile: give it her

(listens; to eat?)

I say shambo sadashiva.

(The names of god themselves

(sings

By Meditation On A Bee, A Larva Easily Becomes A Bee

The taste of silver on her tongue, then

The create world with nothing better to do than mind

She rolled her little ball of dung about with magisterial pomp

With ministerial pride   I wept my own death in life

I pretended I could swim whenever they threw me in

Not otherwise

Where, ever, no

How beauteous was your pretense then

How over the water

Your silver breath did glide

I fathom these words returned damp to me now

So you've never a need for a boat

(Glide, glide)

Lake Dixie Springs springs

We called the movies the show, as in let's go to

Go to, quote you

Mildewed kapok, bream and skin smells

Never before seen bodies of boys

Mine in yellow voile tiny white dots

Knew the names of fabrics then

Fashioned my very limbs

All so you could lie way down

All so I could lie way down

Truth eased of those bodies twined and prone

In solitude, too, I lay waylaid down

You laid way down

The road, good

The burden, good

The girl, good (past tense)

She layed good oh yes

Yes yes, to all that

Springs more

Springs eternal

Limbs

Yes

HEAD-RAG DU-RESS (*DU RON RON*)

i.

Those people have a boat and I don't even have an apartment

Wouldn't 'a car' be more felicitous?

I like to lie all the way down

The wayback: Yes, hell is far

'Fire' is how we say that here

Which side are you on?

I like you sing that Harlan County tune

Djolly Parton

You go to far

Same to you

Ah likeness

ii.

How it feels to put your daughter's picture on a milk carton, I can tell

Coal-miner hell

Is it wishful for my death you are?

The abuse you would be calling and letting out of your mouth

None but an air bubble, for my head was under the water held these
    many years and more, so that I grew shamed I could breathe only air.

Who was it sought to drown?

She wanted to see herself when in my face she looked she wanted a
    mirror her milk to lap

From?

Let's have into

You?

Yes many years later another She saw me with her video eyes, alive

"Can you explain the nature of that pleasure?

No, sir: but I feel it strongly"   How nice to do that turn with you

And now?

Now I sing to her every morning

Before your small clothes?

Before.

We erect hypotheses, to be sure, whenever we punctuate

Some of us to a most stupendous height, plus choice of preposition iii.

When I sing I am on my knees

This pleases?

This pleases; "the pulses on target as after a kiss"

The errant stars the target.

They.

Let us pray for the soul of John Clare

Let us do it today for feeling his words which say

> "And e'en the dearest—
> That I loved the best—
> Are strange—nay, rather stranger
> Than the rest."

How an I feels when an I wants to die

Milk cartons; knowing my heart breaks

How long he lived and forgot in the mad house

Perhaps he was I

"I thought I had a very nice time"

You spare me most kind

I'm more pronounced now it matters

The words of your mouth are the meditation of my heart

Will you say 'beloved' again?

Which if not original remains consummate and unanswerable?

Than any things the lawyers made of glass

Ah

The luck, you know, of Edenhall

Yes: if that glass either break or fall, farewell the luck of Edenhall

Yes: hence, an otolith or ear stone of a fish

Your hence beguiles me yours and truly

I'm very hungry about it, I confess

And so an end to the contagion of diligence

Is heard in the land

However—

Yes?

"I used to lie awake through the whole night and wish for a large pearl"

Oh, and that sort of land is it?

Yes, the poor

I adore you though you are no more

"And still I lie alone"

What difference does it make if I am not vs. am no longer?

The problem of knowing ever

Second nature

Dolly Wilde: there is something sad about being unable to tell the secret of pleasure

Vice Admiral Blandy, commander of the Bikini Atoll nuclear test: I am not
  an atomic playboy

This country ends living things often enough

(   )

Traduce

(tears)

A killing home

( )

The mind of the universe social—

Oh shut up

*Jeannine throws the lamp because Melinda plays Judy Collins because Jeannine's
  old lover used to sing Judy Collins around town*

I miss my Melinda life

One not to have to distance yourself from in order not to bomb civilians

"What I want to know is if she has a piece of hair that does that on the
    other side"

Scientific studies show that 14% of the gulls here in Santa Barbara are lesbian

Of course that wasn't very lady-like for her to lick her hand

Knowing how to do what it is

A reason to like it: because I haven't lost it

The mighty clouds of joy

No more desponding maidens round the willow and the headstone

Never more

Then

Not unknown

Surprise With Fishing Boat Crossing Window Pane, And Ode

> Conversation would have been difficult had he not been alone.
> —Patrick O'Brian, *Treason's Harbour*

I am sitting here right now

Than in all the year else

The sun is setting behind the Olympic Mountains and a sheen is upon
the water

It is the beloved pale blue mirror of evening

At long last I too am allowed to say 'beloved'

'Pretty' was not much and borrowed beside

Looking back on my suffering I see the sign

The sign says 'of happy omen for a favorable issue'

I could not read the sign when I lived in Central Square

The idea of reading time forward

The very

Somebody sang "people can be so unkind"

O Neil, they were good at it there, still I worked very hard

Learned: how to pause briefly on the steps of the post office

One morning my truck door open to snow

The tape player harder to get out than they knew

I make much of there sitting here

In my lap, is it still

Still still

Milk, more—   here—

Where are you, I have your you-then should you want to know now

In case a you can not remember

I can not not remember

Made so?

As you know

Character, a marked wound

And so have lived alive, oh.

FIRST (THE HUNGER)

Only the word?

No, I can touch her too

THE REAL GENESIS PLEASED TO STAND UP

The beautiful day is here again

Bird song and a mist on the water?

All things must pass and return

Darkness only lasts a night time

Better ask Geo. Harrison for lyric assist

And fat boy what ails him with his lash

You digress

I doubt, is what, but the beautiful is day and back

Enough light 'more' to cast

A shadow on the table cloth

On which the ceiling fell

In terrible Iowa-town

You—

Perhaps; back: a junco sings in the lilac

Which nobody's tended the many years

Since an army-wife last in the door yard

De-accessioned bloom

Reminds me of car seats

Good lord

My sweet

And so of hotter than the non-Mississippian can

Know: summer skin by its and others' sweat stuck

Smell the real true amen

A mouthful, you

I did like one and then another too

Will you live there more?

I do. Is the name of the thrill the bleeding heart's rill?

Of note and note depending: yes

Each with its shadow

On the wall of fennel and flowers meet

Shadow wheel true

And tremble

As your hand moves

Onto the page and into our mouths

Word of my heart come fresh to my tongue

May I speak for everyone?

It's alright by me

It is all right bei *you*

Meet and right so to view

Through German, one-eyed, and alone

And touch her missing finger joint

Death, be so unmade

And hear the car horn joyful now

The electric heater in the wall

Its particular call

The bands of light

Above the Sound

I respond

So you abound

In Memoriam Splendor

Can there be more?

Oblate penates her mouth

Can you remember before?

My sister's knee when she was four

Is there room in

You could not say your heart

Then   but look how the cup, too, now bears its shadow

Endure give birth engender—

Défendre de gender

Like the source of its shadow its shadow a-stream

With its likeness

Reflection of darkness

I lived in VT you know

Past unimaginable

In a barn with borrowed windows   a tin stove and flimsy

And no one has taken its life from you

Past knowing

You no longer the ones who do

I would not have it so

Is there a date?

I did not love her

Though loving and planting long rows of vegetables in Chernobyl raining

Frost on my mattress indoors

Your bed sheets on the beets and broccoli outdoors

Water in the Bennington-pottery-seconds cup froze

Time thaws

It hardens views

Tunnels visions

Brown paper dust crawling through the paper mill ducts with a hose

Can you breathe at all with so many in you?

What else would I be doing at all with so many in me?

Maturin Maturin

You know me because you know who I love

Though he doesn't breathe except through you

Lungs not his own, opium, lees

"perishing"

"cabbages, forsooth"

His words on your tongue

Sweet the Demosthenean pebble

Look there will you lick that stone?

Rather will I extend its shadow

With your finger?

You saw

I remember

SPARE

Is it the case?

Accusative?

Nominative: as long as I don't name it we can unknow it?

You are in love with me

I am

I will that you be

I see what you mean

That is the best thing any one ever

Say it to me

THIRD, MIN(D)OR

You are a fountain, are you not?

You like this new free

( )

You are a fountain, are you not?

Fennel   fir   phylactery

( )

That bird sings liquid

There you go

It's true, that was me

OATH: FIRST SWALLOW

i.

My god the light is alive on the water

Behind it the bluff blue

High bluff

Stakes at hand

Cloud banks give it back its wager

It, the low blue land

Won

:ONE

ii.

In the foreground one silver water drop

From a swan-necked faucet

A snake slid by, I sawr it

Yesterday and its yesterday

I walked on sand from beach to land

Leaving the littoral

The snake on sand

Truly seen and said truly

Sandal strap: om guru

Snakes away

Anchors

A chthonic appliance, hum

You bluff

I do

You wanted to say?

The ancient flame yet again

Burns you

I look good in char

You do

She sends me under

You flounder

I right too soon

It's better you stay?

And kiss my sexy doom

Second (what is thirst?)

The shadow gone

The bird its wings spread

MAP

"The sky is what I was telling you about"

And so you touch your head with fingers spread

i.

The sparrow jumped up through the air to the wire

Again your fingers or hair?

I give you both

I raise you and see you too

How I perch on my wire

And drink to you

Bird self-congratulatory?

Air of complacency

How I receive all of your wires: flies through

Each time they charge me I am richer

That, as she said, is the idea

That with a capital T

ol al *elle*

Yes that would be she

You know her then

And now?

The sparrow gone

I think of it too

I see

You do

Now the water entirely gleam

Now the water gleams entirely

ii.

So happy

Hum so

I do

WOE BETIDE

I broke the blue bulb

Is it a disaster beyond measure?

It was a 5 dollar blue bulb

The "Lemnian Horrors" became a proverbial phrase

A world of omens surrounded every man

The women of course had their famous mirrors

Grafted on a Grecian stock every shoot bore Grecian fruit

The Presidential shrub, his formula

Ben Jonson, his Volpone

Et cetera

In deed

The Berliner is Turkish and writes about tulips

Everybody writing about tulips these days

O speculation bubbles and bulbs

O mores: the boy scouts bellow behind his empty house

He wends the road to Sea-Tac

In an airport transport van

I feel Greek chorus-ish

And your hair wants cutting again

Giant shouting voices and branches of broken mess

Hemmed in round about by SUVs wearing kayak headpieces

Where for me the beautiful radish?

Roads in the national forests some more

Trampling down the green-growing

Staining the inner ear and eye

Do you fear your tragic mood?

I do; the raccoons eat oily rags from that garbage can

The reasons for it, too?

The antique grove—the hills and woods of Arcady

Might yet assist me in my need

Were they not rendered in the paper mill whose smokestack plumes the west

If only bellowing might cease

Meditate upon this marguerite, its pink-tinged petals close observe

Har ha ah ha ha reverberates

Would you curse them?

I would but who am I?

Afterward she adds in her beautiful lament...

Wild delight of the Theban maid!

The Larom Linens van is here

To brush the crumbs away

Or at least under the furniture and into the corners

Where also may be found the nail cuttings, tumbleweeds of dust and hair

Of those who've gone before

Hefty smoking harshy maidens

Formed as she exquisitely says of herself to love not hate

Antigone in the state park buried in a bunker

The slamming of many car doors announces the terror that ensues

Americans in RVs

You got it

What will save me?

The snakes auspicious sinuous on the sandy sea-side path?

Not even a slice of bread will save me

Poor poor thing

The past ever present

Absalom Absalom thing

You miss—

I long—

You cared not for the proper definition of nostalgia

Too many words

You wanted only to be there eating the food and hearing the droll words

More imperfect science

Cares not

Cares abounding

Arsenic in all the water

"Sound science"

In 1962 they said the arsenic was a bit much

I believe I remember 1962

*I believe it is not good for us to be always so dismayed, distressed, disgusted
with our government*

The dangers of the unimaginative man

I am water what will save me

I am sadder than I was

What cries?

Nothing to each other

The small boy with the bozo dad and big bleach hair mom waved to you as he got in their bohemah SUV

God is in his heaven

My hair still turning white with the world

SECOND GUES(S)T

i.

She said "love"

She only says "love" when in extremis

When she thinks I say no to her

Abject

What her body feels an argument

Solipsist?

I am persuaded

Which is to say you'd make the same—

Have made the same—

Argument withal, within

I heard it with my skin

ii.

I am beside myself with wanting her

And so in gale force wind you go beside the seaside

Wrack

And ruin for to—

The Titanic may have been good for the iceberg, I thought as I walked

You wore two coats

Three shirts

The details of your mouth on hers lost

Lost on hers?

As you like it

The meaning, however, precise

And deep and deep inside

And like unto the supple wave's belly

Supple belly's wave?

Watching that arcing like coming—

The waves that spend themselves beside your walking

What coming

What's going on?

Marvingaygardens and in the knees weak

Not yr average c⊘w song

Crow song

Drums

Donovan up from the depths: "Way down below the ocean…"

"She made me"

A figure of speech

Which has ever undone you

Figures of speech when in their skin come

To mean mean to meet

THE HOMING DEVICE COMPREHENDED AT LAST

When my god leaves me—

She doesn't leave you

When I don't know she's there, then

And now?

She's here

And now?

How to know which apartment to rent or whether to live with the other
    homeless women in the downtown SRO

No longer pressing

I breathe away the particles of impressing perfection

Permission to not know granted

And inhaled gratefully

What about Holly Springs?

It's all casino boats now

What about Crystal Springs?

The horrible chicken factory

Where to live is less important

At long last

As long as you can sing her

As long as I can sing her

You will be breathing

I will be the breathèd name of god

Some. more. longing.

Some. more. longing.

But this one gets you even closer

To living somewhere I belong

MATRIKA

i.

The newborn swallows in their mud-daub nest

Their cries by the wind so brisk elicit

Yes brisk I never thought I'd say

The word?

The word

Is love

We sing some more

The nictating eyelid of the cat

Appropriate for the third?

Eye thing

See that?

More that some such membrane interposes

Betwixt?

Knowing what the world does

Love

Love

What a word to keep saying

Saking the world into being

For "Thou art That"

To look out into the world from inside

Inside, one's self

Oneself: congruency: wherein

The little eyelid slides back

(The sky again

Again into?

The stuff of seeing sights the eye

Sight prehensile

Touch thereon

The evening's modeling of the cloud

The water's steely fish-scale sheen

I hear the newborn birds cry

ii.

I hear the newborn birds cry

Your heart begin

Be mine again

At last, long last, to bow

Again at last, as last I used

When last you were you

Oddly in Mississippi

Because the forces arrayed against too strong?

My file at the White Citizens Council

They watched you, Klan eyes in heads, on cards

Was I hated?

You were not-known

Everyone who was not their 'us' deemed communist

Northerners don't understand

You can come to understand

Please invite me

Come here

I am—

You—

Last last

iii.

Traffic cones prevented the SUVs wearing kayak headpieces from hemming me in

O Victory; I am too _______ to make adequate reply (which I stole and placed
  them thoughtfully)

What ails you?

I

I understand

You understood

Too tired to be so wrong

Bora-Bora, aye

Solitary confinement and computer disaster

Sigh

No phone

A relief awhile but

A crow pitched a fit to be tied fed

A crow fed it beside the tide

Seafood and a parent at the beach

The 8 a.m. beach

No humans to hide crying from

Frozen now however

Disgruntled by kayak

Disemboweled by

Barreling: the car drives by two toddlers too fast

They were not killed

A thing to be happy about

"I try to be good"

Here comes someone else carrying her own traffic cone

A trend is set

A send is tret

Stet

Stet

(it took a long time to not say *Stetson*...)

( )

KING DUFFUS ARE US

"I sat among poets and among philosophers
Carving fat bacon for the mother of Christ"

The hell you say—says who?

Sylvia

What is Sylvia who is she?

That all the pagans adore her

Vice versa at least

The least of these: whosoever shall do unto

You and yr 'she done me'

Like you better On Riding Oneself Like The Wave One Is?

"Om" spells the face of the water

In 1981 the arroyo water electric and alive

Smell of pale green chamisa and pale pink of horny toad

Who else knows that moment?

'Only you' is insupportably hard for me where you is me

Once one could see through (to)

Oh one Self, not self self self's view

Time a mosaic of the memoried

Mind's mortal mishap: self self self self's view

How the heater renders the middle pane's view wavy

And the power cord dangles down its pole

And a seagull skims the roof peak

And a vine embraces the tree trunk

Just as white paint the power pole

In the mirage-y middle pane

Will you see this Now again?

I was awake in the arroyo and the world came to   came right through

The 'I' gone transparent with congruence

I was all I's

The rivulets glittered in the arroyo water

They moved like moving muscle

Alive: the creature

Yonder, through the moment's door

To See A Flame A Second Flame Is Not Needed

"Nothing unconnected ever occurs, and anything unconnected would instantly perish."

—Emanuel Swedenborg, *Arcana Coelestia 2556*

Isn't it sweet to find someone says what you know beneath words

Found and shown and shone

A morning

The largest orangest moon I've ever seen last night

Sweet and shone too

The three poplars in the sea wind

The fir tree surely a harp of night

This is the feeling of knowing the thing

And the morning?

The feeling of being met in the knowing

And the feeling of knowing being known shared

More being met

Since they get used to being kept in love

More and being, more

THE B&W TV YIELDS A FUZZY HALF-HOUR OF WHAT PROVES TO BE ALLY McBEAL

> "At first we are involved in what is true but not in any goodness of life because of what is true."
> —Emanuel Swedenborg, *Arcana Coelestia 6396*

And so it is we endure the grinding

Of mind against the world

And feel it in the lurch of heart

And low blood pressure system sprinkling the Strait of Juan de Fuca

A gray asperging

Gray an elegant last name for a little girl

And elegant little girl

How come $ always shows up in women's skin?

Beautiful moneyed skin on a little girl even

How come

What a figure hov apeech

Sudden struck British a fruity plummy accent

Comes a one

Now comes _______, legal locution

A jungle gym for the mind, the law

Compassion in the laying down?

I pray the house of lords my soul to keep

A hard pillow

Hard bench

I just understood 'a hard day's night'

I saw you in it yestereve

I donned Robert Downey Jr.'s skin

You bin there

I done that

He is involved

May goodness him behoove

And him relieve

And All The Trees Of The Field Shall Clap Their Hands

Isaiah 55:12

Do you look like that because you are, are you pleased?

I am. My heart is lifted up

You do no heavy lifting

I had not believed it possible though once I strove

And now?

I will be eating six kinds of green for lunch

Once again you yam what you yam

Once and again I enjoy to agree with you

I see that you loved—

It were ever so—

Ivy Compton-Burnett before anyone else

I understand the impulse

Her drift...

She never drifts; rather an eddy compels her

You grew up in such side-stepped violence

The slippers a manner of speaking

Parquet hallway

You take me back to the margarines of yester-year; apologize

I do; pray resume

I resume my pray: Such steppes nothing to one from whom Nothing oozes

How is it possible?

At once the obedient and self-inflicted venom and the rage at being treated so

Another 'compelled'

Another mirror

So was the world her hand mirror

And through it see her own contempt become the face of all

:Stomper stomper stomper blue, I see shame and she is you: the tune she knew

Musical bad magical

Salves my savaged rest

The quarter-rest, lovely

Musical notation, strange and lovely

The Jivanpuri raga

No more the Dorian mode

Spode such a ridiculous name, and unlikable

The British are full of them

How CAN they say 'bickies'?

Their novels so perfectly redolent of themselves (I love them)

It pays to be an island?

Identity needn't defend its pleasures

Mine will be to eat this red pear with two swelling yellow stripes

Dreams inspired by less

Surreptitiously watering plants in a library last night: I dreamed

And also like the giant rose cane in its mysterious animal life

A fourteen foot vegetal creature I loved or thought I was

Good company in dream

Awake I lay and watched it try the air, gentle inquiring, ancient heavy grace

She chopped them all

They'd never bloomed and I loved them

Into bloom

Yes

By recognizing them?

Perhaps

She never even pulled a weed then came out and chopped them down

Well

Well: deep and dark is how common courtesy escapes her

Wave upon wave

When is enough to say goodbye no more?

The clouds above the headlands on the mainlands keep them company

Such things to be able to say

And see

I am, you know

You are, I know

Allowed to say

Starting today?

Starting every day

Hari

Who taketh away the sins of the world

Grant us thy

Pleased

A Shorter History Of Impetus

The hour cometh

And almost now is

I leave again

You do not cry

I pack and unpack and pack and unpack

And look for the next affordable room

It is boring to state fact so

State bird, state flower, so again

Afraid even the sentence will run out like the roof so revisit old sentence

A timed crime

There there

Where where

The paint will peel here without you

Did some blistering thought assist?

No but you participated in your now as you could

Which was that of the two month dwelling

And the toaster with a sign stating how exactly it doesn't work

My toast this morning was delicious

Perhaps you will follow it to Germany

And chew its homeland twelve ways?

Discipular

Scapular

Crepuscular

Unfortunate word

I agree but such a thing never damaged by its signifier

Is there love ('the beautiful parsley') signifying for me? some home?

We have to watch and see

I Was/You Were Not Mistaken In Me

I say Bora-Bora

Somewhat nostalgically

In Water, The Self Of The Water

I lived somewhere some weeks

Put found things on the windowsill, just like dwelling

Hid the ugly rug

Stuffed the hole in the wall

Allowed more than when first I came

Allowed as how you are willing to undo certain Pain

My will subject to my mind's deep well

As how, as when limpid Printemps...

As when swift-footed somebody—like me, beside the wine-dark sea

Every leaving death to you

Every leaving tree

To cleave the earth you grew from

To grow whole from what is cleft

Inscribing each leaf with unspeakable grief

In sorrow, rather, to turn the face earth-ward

When packing-boxes loom in corners

Then I remembered words and felt I had been saved

Surely you exaggerate?

Overstate, perhaps, or mis—: I remembered transformations past

And felt deliverance possible

The posture and the gesture

Head bowed, hand rowed across page

It furthers one to cross this great water

The water of Now

For the adjustment can be made only in the present

For in it I am undone by an upwell of longing

Undone?

A wind ripples the great water

Hinders?

Hinterlands intimated and intimate

The wish for home

For the moving that is not the packing of boxes and the viewing of rooms

The anxious counting of dollars again and again

Now as forever or some such

"Somewhat"

Mr. Verdi said that

I believe he did

Belief breathes on the face of the waters

Grace moves over, belief makes off

Do you care for this distinction?

The one lovely cloud over the wide sea

Rain or shadow or its being seen: grace

Makes to waves or not: belief

The depths from whence arise

The letters of the alphabet

Break the surface as you breathe

Speaking breath: some words into some ear

Let us go this slowly always

I seemed to in the streaming South

And so the steamy night along

So long

You were long reviled there

And elsewhere, sure; mistook the why

So you could write: hier ist kein Warum

And still there dwell

Marianne and her mother gone to Terezin

Deathcamp survivors a national treasure

Pearls before swine

Dissolved in champagne?

Cleopatra another tear-loser

Another Roxy Music song

Over the dam of memory

The waters are rising?

While 'here' is drought: salmon can't get there either

They know where to go though

They smell where as they go

They know?

They don't know more than you do

Nor try the harder: at the windowed salmon ladder, cried

A public spectacled

I papered over the window: don't see here the world's shame

I hear 'hier'

A concentration camp for 'nature'?

Seems a bit offensively much

Analogy and analoger as capitalist: hell bent for profit

For leather, hell-bent for, is that a figure?

Index, finger

Point, blame, blamer

PURVIEW

I say Bora-Bora

And so you are

Of God, the bridge across

I say Bora-Bora for I am brought across

The ocean of the world. You are

Am (You practice on me

Art (I practice

That

That

Sounds the many in the One

I love the little thing so hard

I'm made of names

I do I love when somebody I love be having what I got

Of God: mainsail topsail

Patrick O'Brian

Arbor, platelet, satchidananda

"That which gives anything pleasant its ability to please"

Astonishing me

Mississippi's Junior Miss sat in front of me alphabetically in junior high

You painted a mustache on her giant highway billboard face one night

It said 'Brookhaven, home of' her

Could not be borne by un-homely you

She called me 'Li' once she spoke to me

Li Po

"Lila"

Names then you did not know

Many and many

Did not give up

Multitudes still I dream

Have come to be in me

Sing through

"Anahata nada"

Unsounded sound that sounds the worlds

I, thou, art, That: stage directions

Roles, lines, the same as names

"Lilarasa"

May I mean every word I says

Oh ability to please

"Baby take thet there jar of fig preserves cause I wants you

To care a little something for me"

NOTES

"I salute Shri Guru...": Verse 43, Guru Gita, as sung in Gurumayi's ashrams

"Love said...": George Herbert's *Love (III)*

"Which side are you on?": Coal miners' song

"I thought I had a very nice time": Title of my poem published in *New Review of Literature* and *Experimental Theology*

"And still I lie alone": (*ego de mono kateudo*) Sappho's poem, "The Moon Has Set..."

"Where for me the beautiful parsley?": Ancient Greek musical inscription from funeral stele

"Matrika": Matrika Shakti—(Sanskrit, lit. the power of the mother) The goddess as the form of the sounds of the Sanskrit alphabet, the creative force of the universe, the power of letters and words

"I sat among poets...": Sylvia Townsend Warner

"Hier ist kein Warum": Here is no why; of the death camps

"Satchidananda": (Sanskrit, lit. absolute existence, consciousness, and bliss) The nature/experience of the Consciousness that is the Absolute, aka the *That* in Thou art That.

"Lila": (Sanskrit, lit. sport or play) Existence or reality as the play of Consciousness, of Shiva and Shakti

"Rasa": Sanskrit, savor, taste, juice, nectar

ACKNOWLEDGEMENTS

The Imagined Snake Is The Sport Of The Rope: *Ploughshares*

Surcingle, Fuller: *VOLT*

Oath: First Swallow: *Colorado Review*

Surprise With Fishing Boat…And Ode; By Meditation On A Bee…; Head-Rag Du-ress (*du ron ron*): *Interim*

Second Gues(s)t; The Homing Device Comprehended At Last: *New American Writing*

A Shorter History of Impetus: *Weber: The Contemporary West*

Thanks to Centrum and to the Helene Wurlitzer Foundation, for beautiful time and space, and to the Boomerang Foundation, all of which made this book possible.

My boundless and abiding gratitude to Gurumayi, whose grace makes time and space avail.

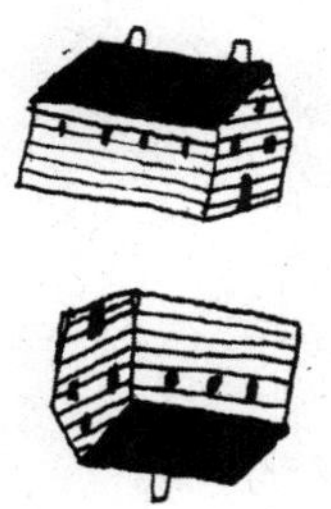